SandCastle™

Let's Measure

WHAT
in the
WORLD
is a
GALLON?

Mary Elizabeth Salzmann

Published by ABDO Publishing Company, 8000 West 78th Street, Edina, Minnesota 55439.
Copyright © 2009 by Abdo Consulting Group, Inc. International copyrights reserved in all countries.
No part of this book may be reproduced in any form without written permission from the publisher.
SandCastle™ is a trademark and logo of ABDO Publishing Company.

Printed in the United States.

Editor: Pam Price
Curriculum Coordinator: Nancy Tuminelly
Cover and Interior Design and Production: Colleen Dolphin, Mighty Media
Photo Credits: BananaStock Ltd., Colleen Dolphin, Eyewire Images, iStockphoto/Jon Woidka,
iStockphoto/Stefan Klein, Shutterstock
Illustrations: Colleen Dolphin

Library of Congress Cataloging-in-Publication Data

Salzmann, Mary Elizabeth, 1968-

 What in the world is a gallon? / Mary Elizabeth Salzmann.

   p. cm. -- (Let's measure)

 ISBN 978-1-60453-164-0

1. Weights and measures--Juvenile literature. I. Title.

 QC90.6.S25 2009

 530.8--dc22

                    2008008203

SandCastle™ books are created by a professional team of educators, reading specialists, and content developers
around five essential components—phonemic awareness, phonics, vocabulary, text comprehension, and fluency—
to assist young readers as they develop reading skills and strategies and increase their general knowledge. All books
are written, reviewed, and leveled for guided reading, early reading intervention, and Accelerated Reader® programs
for use in shared, guided, and independent reading and writing activities to support a balanced approach to literacy
instruction. The SandCastle™ series has four levels that correspond to early literacy development in young children.
The levels are provided to help teachers and parents select appropriate books for young readers.

SandCastle Level: Transitional

Emerging Readers
(no flags)

Beginning Readers
(1 flag)

Transitional Readers
(2 flags)

Fluent Readers
(3 flags)

SandCastle™ would like to hear from you! Please send us your comments or questions.

sandcastle@abdopublishing.com

www.abdopublishing.com

GALLON

A gallon is a unit of measurement. A large milk jug holds 1 gallon.

Gallons are used to measure volume. When you know how much a gallon is, you can find out how much of something there is.

The abbreviation for gallon is gal.

1 gallon is the same as 1 gal.

Many things come in containers that hold 1 gallon. When they are empty, you can use the containers to measure the amount of other things.

gallon of milk

gallon of paint

gallon of ice cream

JASON CAN MEASURE!

Jason helps out around the house. He does a different job each day. He uses a milk jug to measure how much water he uses for each chore.

On Monday Jason cleans the fishbowl.
He gives his goldfish fresh water.
The fishbowl holds 3 gallons.

+ +

On Tuesday Jason mops the kitchen floor. He fills a large bucket with water. The bucket holds 5 gallons.

+   +   +

+

On Wednesday Jason helps wash the dishes. He fills one side of the kitchen sink with water. It holds 4 gallons.

+ + +

On Thursday Jason waters the plants. He fills the watering can. It holds 1 gallon of water.

On Friday Jason puts water in the birdbath. The birdbath holds 2 gallons.

+

On Saturday Jason washes the car. His friend Richard helps. They fill two buckets with water. Each bucket holds 5 gallons. Together they use 10 gallons of water. $(5 + 5 = 10)$

On Sunday Jason doesn't have chores. He and Richard play in the swimming pool. It holds 50 gallons of water! That's 10 buckets!

+ + + + +

+ + + +

MEASURING EVERY DAY!

Alyssa holds the paint can while her dad paints the fence. The can holds 1 gallon of paint.

PAINT

Gavin likes to drink milk every day. His mom buys 2 gallons of milk each week for their family.

Brooke gives
Cosmo a bath.
The washtub holds
8 gallons of water.

Cole's family stopped to buy gas on the way to his soccer game. The gas pump measured the gas. They bought 11 gallons of gas.

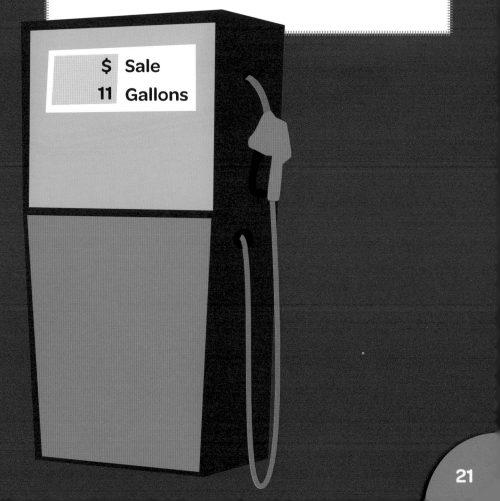

$ Sale
11 Gallons

MEASURING IS FUN!

How many gallons of water does it take to fill up your bathtub? What else can you measure in gallons?

LET'S MEASURE!

Which of these things is about one gallon?

(answer: white jug)

22

MORE ABOUT MEASURING

Volume

16 cups = 1 gallon

Sometimes you use part of a cup or gallon to measure something.

The recipe needs 1 and 1/2 cups of brown sugar.

We bought a half gallon of milk at the store.

GLOSSARY

amount – how much there is of something.

bucket – a container that has a handle and is used to hold or carry liquids or solids.

chore – a regular job or task, such as cleaning your room.

container – something that other things can be put into.

empty – having nothing inside.

measurement – a piece of information found by measuring.

pump – a device that forces liquid or gas from one place to another.

unit – an amount used as a standard of measurement.

volume – the amount a container can hold.